BEER AND SPIRITS

HAUNTED HOSTELRIES
OF BEDFORDSHIRE

BEER & SPIRITS

HAUNTED
HOSTELRIES
OF

BEDFORDSHIRE

by
Julie E. Bounford PhD

with an original ghost story by
Trevor Bounford

Gottahavebooks
16 Middle Street
Great Gransden
SG19 3AD
United Kingdom

ISBN 978-0-9933781-7-1

Cover and page layout design by Bounford.com

Map and images © 2018 Bounford.com

Contents

Illustrations

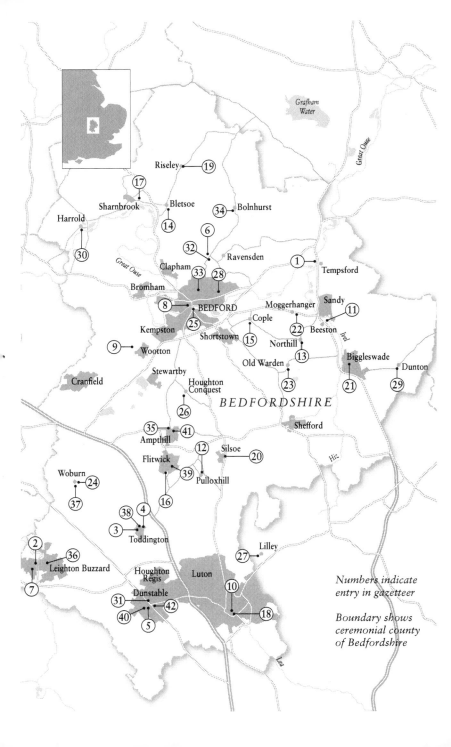

Grafham Water

Great Ouse

Riseley • ⑲

⑰
Sharnbrook
◇ Bletsoe
Harrold
⑭
⑭
Bolnhurst
⑥
⑰
Harrold
⑭
⑭
Bolnhurst
⑥
⑯
⑭
⑭
⑭
Bolnhurst
⑥
⑯
⑳

Great Ouse

Clapham
Ravensden
① Tempsford
⑫
㉝ ㉘
Bromham
⑧ • BEDFORD
Moggerhanger Sandy
㉒ ⑪
Kempston
㉕
Cople Beeston
Shortstown ⑮ Northill Ivel
⑨ Wootton ⑬
Old Warden Biggleswade Dunton
Cranfield Stewartby ㉓ ㉑ ㉙
Houghton
Conquest BEDFORDSHIRE
㉖ Shefford
㉟ ㊶
Ampthill ⑫ Silsoe
Flitwick ⑫ ⑳
Woburn ㊴ Pulloxhill Hiz
㉔ ⑯
㊲
㊳ ④
③ Toddington
Leighton Buzzard Lilley
② ㊱ Houghton ㉗
Regis Luton
⑦ ㉛ Dunstable
㊵ ㊷ ⑩
⑤ ⑱

Lea

Numbers indicate
entry in gazetteer

Boundary shows
ceremonial county
of Bedfordshire

Introduction

I urge you to visit Bedfordshire, a county of 'detail rather than grand gesture', with variety 'greater in architecture than in scenery' (Mackay 1987; Pevsner 1968). Many will agree it is a county with hidden depths that, upon closer inspection, reveal the most intriguing stories and characters. The shire's hostelries, having witnessed all manner of life and death over the centuries, prove to be no exception as they offer the possibilities of mysterious encounters that will defy rational explanation.

Drawing from various published accounts of paranormal activity in Bedfordshire, I have packed a lot of information into this slim volume, including a map, a gazetteer so you can find over forty locations with reported activities, and an original ghost story by Trevor Bounford designed to put you in the right frame of mind for spectral encounters.

Julie E. Bounford PhD

———————————

Please note that public houses often change their function, or may even be closed down and converted into private residences. Some of our examples are no longer pubs but are included out of historical interest. Please respect people's privacy. I encourage you to seek out only those locations that are still open for business.

Always check before visiting – or expect the unexpected!

GHOSTLY GAZETTEER

Brush up on your knowledge of haunted Bedfordshire hostelries. The gazetteer entries are listed in alphabetical order, with the name, location and postcode provided for each operating establishment. Every entry has a brief account of the reported ghostly activity, with longer descriptions and a small illustration provided in some cases.

---

1. Anchor Lodge

Great North Road, Tempsford, Sandy, SG19 2AS

Reported activity: heavy footsteps in the bar, rattling pots and pans in the kitchen, orbs, and jangling coat hangers in the wardrobe.

---

2. The Bedford Arms

(formerly The Corbet Arms, now closed)
Old Road, Linslade, Leighton Buzzard

Reported activity: an elderly woman standing over guests as they sleep in their room, the sound of a woman's voice and her dress swishing along the carpet.

---

3. The Bedford Arms

(now closed)
High Street, Toddington

Reported activity: sighting of a Cavalier standing by the fireplace, and a grieving seafaring captain dressed in a red and blue tunic. Mourning his murdered wife and child, he took his own life in an upstairs room.

4. The Bell

Market Square, Toddington, LU5 6BP

Reported activity: this is a sad tale of the demise of a pretty girl and subsequent hauntings. It is said that the landlord's daughter in the 1850s had a temperament that could be easily provoked, that she was prone to violent outbursts. Observing any early signs of a temper, the landlord would lock his daughter in another room (the kitchen or a room upstairs), leaving her to cool off. For an hour or so she would crash around, venting her spleen until eventually, she had calmed down. On one occasion, after just few minutes, a strange silence ensued and sadly, when the landlord unlocked the door, he discovered that his daughter had died. How, we will never know. Perhaps she had some sort of undiagnosed condition whereby she suffered from seizures. It seems that an apparition of the girl has been seen only once and the temperature of one room upstairs is constantly chilled all year round. On the other hand, a poltergeist has, on occasions, been very active. Pots and pans have been thrown across the kitchen, and pictures torn from walls. Glasses have been broken, loud bangs have been heard, shoulders have been tapped and doors have been opened and closed in empty rooms.

The Bell

5. The Black Horse

(now closed)
West Street, Dunstable
Reported activity: sighting in the bar of a headless man from the Civil War period, lights being turned off and on, and the overnight undoing of any attempt at tidying up before bedtime.

6. The Blacksmith Arms

(now The Curry Mansion)
Bedford Road, Ravensden, MK44 2RA
Reported activity: banging doors, a push in the stomach by something or someone unseen, a drop in temperature, cold draughts and strange coloured lights.

7. The Buckingham Arms

(formerly The Railway Tavern)
Old Road, Linslade, Leighton Buzzard, LU7 2RB
Reported activity: many sounds of slamming doors, footsteps running up and down the stairs and of barrels being moved around in the cellar. In the early morning the front garden gate unlatches itself and someone is heard walking up the path and then knocking loudly on the front door.

8. The Bull Nosed Rat

(now the Wodka Live Bar and formerly The Chameleon, Que Paso) St. Paul's Square, Bedford, MK40 1SL
Reported activity: various phenomena following the discovery of 30 bodies during a renovation (it was built on the site of a graveyard), such as a bottle depositing itself into a bin, a ghostly cat spotted upstairs and a cold spot by the exit door.

9. The Chequers Inn,

Hall End Rd, Wootton, MK43 9HP

Reported activity: a vanishing ghost, possibly that of a former groomsman who sadly died under the wheels of a coach.

10. The Cork and Bull

(now Bar 32) Cumberland Street, Luton, LU1 3BW

Reported activity: the ghost of Ann, murdered at the pub many years ago, has been seen in the pub and in the street outside. She has been known to throw stools across the room and to shake tables. Customers, whom she has touched, have talked with her, unaware that she was an apparition.

11. The Cross

(now closed)

High Road, Beeston, Sandy

Reported activity: whiskey bottles falling off the shelves, the beer gas turned off, the front door bolted, ladies locked in the bathroom, and snooker chalk levitating.

12. The Cross Keys

High Street, Pulloxhill, MK45 5HB

Reported activity: according to paranormal investigations, this tavern has several ethereal visitors including a grey lady who appears to sit near the fireplace where a strange atmosphere may linger. In 2003, a spiritualist, Joan Dancer, saw her there, looking sad whilst busy crocheting. Joan believes this lady was called Mary and she had three children, Jane, Meg and William. Mary died at the age of 56 in 1874. Another figure at the Cross Keys has been recognised as a former landlord who died there. He still visits, wearing a brown 1930s suit. Others include a fair-haired soldier called Harry Atkins (wearing a red uniform, a pillbox hat and shiny shoes), a farmhand called George (wearing a crew-necked shirt and buttoned breeches), a Cavalier and a man who had drowned in a nearby pond. In 2003, the landlord's dog would always walk around the edges of the restaurant, even at night, to avoid a haunting 'power line' that went straight across the room. Cold spots, strange blue and red lights, energies and sounds such as a baby crying when no children were on the premises, have been witnessed. In 1986, Joan Dancer was visiting with a friend and they both saw her teaspoon float off her saucer, only to slowly descend of its own accord into her lap!

The Cross Keys

13. The Crown

Ickwell Road, Northill, SG18 9AA

Reported activity: sighting of former monks from the Order of the Knights Hospitaller, on the stairs, and gliding across the car park onto the lawn and into the woods (the pub was a vicarage connected to a local monastery). The presence of a warm spot on the floor behind the bar.

14. The Falcon Inn

Rushden Road, Bletsoe, MK44 1QN

Reported activity: in the eighteenth century this coaching inn was a regular stop for soldiers as they marched from London to face the Bonnie Prince Charlie's Highlanders. It may well have been during this period when a young ostler unfortunately died after a fall from the hayloft. People feel uncomfortable in the bottle store, which used to be the old stables. His ghost can be seen in the kitchen and the grounds, and his presence is said to be responsible for the strange disappearance – and reappearance – of certain items. But that is not all. A poltergeist, apparently with a keen sense of 'everything in its place' tidied up a chef's bedroom, picking up the clothes and shoes she had strewn all over the floor. Heavy footsteps have been heard pacing up and down the upstairs corridor. Back downstairs, keys, bottles, glasses and books were not put away but thrown at the staff, and bottles would regularly fall off the shelves. Bookshelves were seen to float across a room and on one occasion, a glass decanter was moved across the bar and its stopper lifted by invisible hands, as witnessed by several people. Whilst alone in the restaurant, staff have had things thrown at them, and their name called.

The Falcon

15. The Five Bells

Northill Road, Cople, MK44 3TU

Reported activity: the sighting of a man with a pigtail (possibly a sailor) sitting by the fireplace, smoking a clay pipe.

16. Flitwick Manor

Church Rd, Flitwick, MK45 1AE

Reported activity: repair or restoration work to an old building often appears to arouse a dormant spirit. Located on a site first occupied as a Roman settlement, the current Manor (built in the late seventeenth century), was owned and occupied by the Brooks family from 1789 until 1934, when a cousin, Robert Adolphus Lyall, inherited it. In the 1950s it was purchased by television and film director Anthony Gilkison and in the 1980s it was converted into a restaurant. It is now a Hallmark Hotel.

A wooden door to a hidden room (possibly servants' quarters) was discovered near the roof during some renovation works. This portentous discovery noticeably changed the Manor's atmosphere and appeared to disturb the ghostly spirit of an old woman who has made herself known to staff and customers alike. Appearing in people's bedrooms, her presence would be accompanied either by the sensation of a heavy weight on the bed and a refreshing hand on the forehead, or by a strong sense of anguish and distress. On one sighting, the old woman appeared to be crying. She has been known to also appear in the upstairs corridor, switch lights on and off, and knock on doors, which were sometimes unlocked by a spiritual presence. She has also appeared downstairs in the morning room. A former manager who had many encounters with the old woman, knew when the ghost was

Flitwick Manor

present because she could see an impression on the cushions, as though someone were sitting there. Her appearance would also sometimes be accompanied by the scent of rose perfume. The ghost of a girl has been spotted in the dining room and is thought by a psychic to be called Lucy.

Who is the old woman? Described as a white-haired lady in Victorian dress, she could be either former resident Mrs Brooks, who refuses to leave the house after her daughter's untimely demise in 1848, or former housekeeper Mrs Banks, who was said to have been dismissed by the Lyall family when they suspected her of poisoning one of their sons. Sadly, he died. Perhaps Mrs Banks had occupied the hidden room when it was servants' quarters.

They say that an exorcism was conducted at the Manor in late nineteenth century. If so, it was to no avail. Over the years investigators have detected various elements of paranormal activity such as a powerful magnetic field in one of the bedrooms, indicating the presence of a strong energy.

A clairvoyant had a disturbing impression of a dead woman laying in a bath filled with blood. Less distressing were orbs of light and a man's face at a window. A clock fell off the kitchen wall and saucepans lids flew out of cupboards, landing noisily on the tiled floor. Who or whatever they may be, the spectres at Flitwick Manor have been most active.

17. The Fordham Arms

Templars Way, Sharnbrook, MK44 1PX

Reported activity: formerly The Railway Hotel, this inn reportedly hosts as many as six phantoms including a person wearing a cape seen in the bar, only to disappear through a wall where there was once a doorway. A visit by the Anglia Paranormal Investigation Society some years ago ended up with a disturbing experience for a team member who had invited the presence to make itself known. Immediately, an unseen energy rushed straight through him, leaving a fierce wind in its wake felt by another investigator. Energy was not the only thing that flew around as objects such as a plastic ice cream scoop have been know to fly across the cellar.

The Fordham Arms

18. The Four Horseshoes

Park Street, Luton, LU1 3EU

Reported activity: a gust of cold air accompanied by the sound from the cellar of money being counted, possibly by the ghost of William Clifford, who was the owner in 1876 when the original pub building burned down. After the fire his body was found by the back door, clutching the night's takings.

19. The Fox and Hounds

High Street, Riseley, MK44 1DT

Reported activity: the sound of coughing and of footsteps. Lights turned off and on. The sighting of a young nurse, sadly run over by a coach in front of the tavern. Her body was brought inside after the accident. She has been seen by the fireplace and in the car park.

20. The George

High Street, Silsoe, MK45 4EP

Reported activity: whilst this former coaching inn (dating back to 1838 – a former building dates back to the early seventeenth century) may no longer be a public house, it seems fitting to relate the sad tale of Lady Elizabeth Grey of nearby Wrest Park. It is said that Elizabeth had been hiding out at the inn for two weeks with her lover, a young coachman. When discovered by her father, they attempted to elope. Tragically, their coach crashed into a lake and they both drowned. Over the years Elizabeth has been seen and heard by staff and by customers. The inn had been exorcised in 1959 but the strange activity continued. In 2003, a medium led an investigation at the inn and declared she had made contact with the spirits of Elizabeth and her lover.

The George, Silsoe

There were reportedly five ghosts occupying the premises. A member of staff was reported as saying that he had some very odd experiences whilst living there. For example, he heard the kettle boiling in the kitchen and upon investigation, discovered that whilst the kettle was hot, it was also unconnected to the power supply. In the early 1990s some workmen opened up the lounge fireplace and discovered an old gravestone with the word, 'widow' engraved upon it. There is no explanation of its presence, although in 1625 a stranger died at the old George tavern and in 1751, the inn was visited by three highwaymen, one of whom was subsequently shot in the head soon after.

21. The Golden Pheasant

High St, Biggleswade, SG18 0JH
Reported activity: the sound of footsteps upstairs, supposedly a ghost named Maurice, and of a woman singing in the bar.

22. The Guinea

Bedford Road, Moggerhanger, MK44 3RG
Reported activity: sighting of a small boy called Benjamin

from the mid-eighteenth century in breeches, sitting by the fire. Said to have hated the cold, sadly he died young. He appeared to have had problems with his legs and would often stumble, as testified by a visiting psychic. He liked to play tricks and on one occasion it seems he caused an old framed nineteenth century stamp book to fly across the bar as though thrown, witnessed by several customers.

23. The Hare and Hounds

Old Warden, SG18 9HQ

Reported activity: a 'happy' presence in a room known as The Chapel, and the sighting of a woman in the bar and upstairs.

24. The Inn or The Woburn Hotel

(formerly The Saint George, The George, The Bedford Arms)
George Street, Woburn, MK17 9PX

Reported activity: sighting of a man sitting by the fireplace, smoking a clay pipe, wearing a hat and smock, accompanied by his dog, and the vaporous presence of a lady.

25. The King's Arms

St. Mary's Street, Bedford, MK42 0AS

Reported activity: some public houses have been used as mortuaries in the past. It is said that a coffin-shaped trap door above the bar at this sixteenth century tavern was used to lower bodies from the room above. Mortuary or not, the hauntings may be a case of 'upstairs, downstairs' as two apparitions were reported to occupy different parts of the building. Staff had mentioned feeling the presence of someone behind them whilst working in the cellar. A spectre seen down there clearly

The Kings Arms

wants to make himself useful, despite his tendency to throw beer barrels. Described as an older gentleman in a white short-sleeved shirt, he has been known to strip down the beer taps after they have been cleaned and left to dry; a complicated task for anyone, never mind a ghost. Whilst upstairs, the floorboards have creaked under the footsteps of someone unseen, though some say it is a young man. Whatever it was set the resident dog barking. On one occasion old blacksmith nails were flung by someone unseen at a customer in the bar, and on another, a woman and her children who were staying overnight discovered in the morning that they had been left rings beside their beds by persons unknown.

26. The Knife and Cleaver

(formerly The Butcher's Arms) Houghton Conquest, MK45 3LA
Reported activity: pages of the bookings diary turning by themselves and a ghostly hand appearing over the barman's shoulder as he looked on. Cold draughts and tugging at a customer's jacket sleeve, a pump badge flying off the handle, and a cushion flipping over by itself.

27. The Lilley Arms

West Street, Lilley, LU2 8LN

Reported activity: glimpses of three ghosts; Old Tom, an old woman and a lady named Frances.

28. The Lincoln Arms

(Goldington Hall – now closed)
Goldington Green, Bedford

Reported activity: sighting of a lady in Victorian dress on the landing and the sound of a small girl walking around upstairs.

29. The March Hare

High Street, Dunton, SG18 8RN

Reported activity: sighting in a doorway of a tall ghost that subsequently vanished.

30. The Oakley Arms

High St, Harrold, MK43 7BH

Reported activity: sighting of a former landlord, Dan Orpin, who ran the pub in the 1930s and '40s, sitting in the public bar, sometimes smoking a cigarette or sipping a pint.

31. The Old Sugar Loaf

High Street, North Dunstable, LU6 1LA

Reported activity: the ghost of a man who hanged himself in one of the upper rooms.

32. The Old White Lion

(now closed)
Bedford Road, Ravensden

Reported activity: sighting of a woman who previously lived at the cottage and a rose bush in the garden that blooms a single rose every year on 22 May, the birthdate of Elizabeth Peacock (who died in 1881), the daughter and then the wife of previous landlords, Thomas Bazley & George Peacock.

33. The Park
Kimbolton Road, Bedford, MK40 2PF
Reported activity: sighting of a Second World War solider who died when the building was being used as a hospital.

34. The Plough
Kimbolton Road, Bolnhurst, MK44 2EX
Reported activity: sighting of a ghost called Cedric, a former farm worker with a large tummy, wearing a white shirt, a waistcoat, trousers tied with string and big boots.

35. The Queen's Head
Woburn Street, Ampthill, MK45 2HP
Reported activity: sighting of a man wearing eighteenth century clothes.

36. The Ram Inn
(now closed)
Leighton Buzzard
Reported activity: sighting of a ghost and poltergeist activity followed by an exorcism in the 1990s.

37. The Royal Oak
George Street, Woburn, MK17 9PY

Reported activity: sensed but not observed – e.g. cold spots, slamming doors, turning off taps to the beer pumps and taking flowers from vases.

38. The Sow and Pigs

(now closed)

Church Square, Toddington

Reported activity: sighting of a ghost, a man in a cloak who appeared in the gentleman's toilet alongside those using the facilities, and asked them to 'move over'.

39. The Swan

Dunstable Close, Flitwick, MK45 1HP

Reported activity: a ghost who likes to hide people's belongings, especially those of new members of staff.

40. The Victoria

West Street, Dunstable, LU6 1ST

Reported activity: sighting of a young stable hand who haunts the rear of the building where the stables once stood. It is said that he seriously injured his hand and he appears with a bandaged arm.

41. The White Hart

Dunstable Street, Ampthill, MK45 2NG

Reported activity: doors closing by themselves, at first slowly until they are within two centimetres of closing, and then slamming. A bar window flying open against the prevailing wind, a spirit who likes a certain door to be kept open, the sighting of a gentleman in a top hat walking in through the

The White Hart

main door and then vanishing, glasses moving around the bar during the night. In 2004, the hotel was subjected to an investigation by the Luton Paranormal Society. The results included demonic laughter in Edith Bray's Chamber, recorded on an audiotape, a sound that was not heard when the recording was being made; a series of red, purple and white lights in the corner of the Red Chamber, and a woman's voice in Room Four, shouting, 'Get out, Get out!'

42. The White Swan Inn

High Street, Dunstable, LU6 3SF

Reported activity: sighting of a figure walking through an empty bar, spotted by staff monitoring the security camera but failing to materialise on film.

Who's There?

by Trevor Bounford

THERE ARE ANY number of public houses rumoured to be haunted throughout the length and breadth of the land. No doubt, some tales are deliberately devised or enhanced to draw in custom. Obviously, a pub with a 'resident' ghost, with a plausible story to back it up, could elevate the establishment's status to some degree, although that may not always be the case. The idea of a ghost may have the opposite effect on trade, and many publicans, aware of this detriment, will play down, or even deny, the evidence of a 'presence' on the premises.

These facts may seem quite obvious to anyone devoting time to reflection on the topic but it is undoubtedly the case that very many pubs, and hotels, have, at some time or another, been recorded has having visitations from one or more otherworldly beings. Perhaps this too is not surprising as these are public venues, places existing for the very purpose of hosting visitors of all kinds. Furthermore, the consumption of alcohol has undoubtedly contributed to the origination, not only of the tales, but also the events that inspired them.

Thus, it is quite a task for the discerning 'ghost researcher' to sift through the dross and the fanciful in an effort to establish the veracity of any legend, whatever the 'venue' – inn, house, castle or hut. And there are very determined researchers to this day engaged in this serious study. These are not 'ghost hunters' as might be portrayed by the entertainment business. No, these are sober students of the super-natural, spending their lives poring over attested documents. Such research, when considered of serious import, then leads to exploration in the field, if possible, with carefully planned and systematic investigation.

There is one group in particular, not a formal society as such, but a number of individuals whose paths have crossed in their pursuits. This is a most respected and close-knit group of determined people. Through the careful, and usually generous, sharing of information, researches have been advanced. Of course, these people have no interest in the commercial exploitation of their work. They do not publish popular guides, or contribute to any sensationalist publications. In fact, they rarely share the information gleaned with the proprietors of establishments hosting apparitions. Some private publications are produced and shared but even then, there is rarely more than a handful of copies produced and these are cautiously distributed, passing from trusted hand to trusted hand.

Jon Spelling was a member, if that term can be used for such an informal association, of that group. It is not known how many others would have been associated but they comprised a seemingly random selection of individuals, male and female – retired academics, a former Anglican bishop, at least two priests, a school-master and a doctor amongst them. Mostly middle-aged at least, Jon being one of the youngest at 37 years old. He, himself, had had direct contact with only three or four of this circle, and had only actually met one other – through whom he became associated. And it was this one, who served as a sort of central contact, whom Jon telephoned one day.

As usual, the telephone rang several times before the recorded answer service activated.

'Gordon Gillman is unable to take –' but Jon was too excited to wait.

'Gordon, sorry, I know you are there, please pick up,' he managed, then gasped and swallowed, 'Sorry, but it's urgent. I need to check something with you, please.'

He hoped he hadn't sounded too excited – that was not how serious researchers behaved, of course. But containing his excitement after such a momentous discovery would surely have been an issue for anyone.

The recorded message had continued while he spoke. It ended and he paused, holding the receiver away from his ear, wondering already if he might call another associate but could not think of any living name – two previous contacts, fellow members, as it were, had passed away, not unexpectedly, within the past few weeks. He half-smiled as the thought of contacting either through a medium came to mind.

'Hello?' It was Gordon's hesitant voice on the line.

'Gordon, thank goodness. Listen, did you get Graham's widow to send you Alban's tome – you said he'd promised it and –'

'Fine thanks. And yourself?'

Jon wondered if Gordon had heard him, then realized he'd been remiss.

'Oh, sorry. I should have asked. How are you?' he paused momentarily, 'Of course, you had the op., last week, wasn't it? How did it go?'

'It was last month – early last month – and it went well, thank you,' Gordon's familiar, ponderous delivery helped steady Jon somewhat.

'Anyway, I wasn't expecting you to worry about my health,' Jon was nodding and smiling as the deliberated words passed down the line, 'It's just customary to start a conversation with a little courteous enquiry, unless you're some blasted electronic device. Mind you, even them things can seem to show a little interest in a person.'

'Okay, okay. Point taken. And quite rightly made. And I do care about your health and well-being. Now the hip's done, we can go for that beer we promised.'

'But that was not the purpose of your call, I gather.'

Jon could picture the lugubrious features that so suited the diction. And he knew he was being teased. Nevertheless, as he drew breath, he realised his heart was pumping faster than it should do during a normal conversation. Then, this was not a normal conversation. What he wanted to discuss was big, very big. At least, if he was right, it was.

'Alban's book – did you …' he tailed off, not sure now how to ask delicately. After all, he had no idea how close Gordon might have been to Graham. 'Did Graham's …, was their a will … or something?' he tried.

'I am holding in my hand, one pristine copy, well, not that pristine, but not that bad considering it is one hundred and seventy years old, and has been very well thumbed. Actually, probably as much fingered as thumbed. Got the look of a car mechanic's manual about it in places.'

Jon felt a wave of relief.

'Gordon, I need … I'd like to …'

No matter how he tried, he realised he couldn't ask what he really wanted. It simply wasn't proper, in the circumstances. Whether Gordon and Graham had been close or not, the man had just inherited one of the rarest, and most authoritative, texts on the subject of 'ghost hunting'. He despised that term, they all did, those seriously engaged in serious research, but it was now in popular usage, and it did describe what they were doing, to a great extent.

'The Ghost-Hunter General's very own publication of his collected notes,' said Gordon.

Jon was astonished. He had never heard Gordon use those words. Alban – Gerhard Alban – was so revered by all who knew his work. No-one with proper involvement in 'spectral investigation', the rather feeble officially adopted term that sort of described what they did, would consider using the phrase 'Ghost-Hunter General'.

'I've never heard you use that … those words,' Jon was so

struck, he forgot for the moment the urgency of his mission.

'It's what Graham wrote on the card that came with it. I think he was being ironic – or maybe taking the piss. He did get a bit frivolous about it all in his later years. Mind you, if you get to ninety seven years old, you're allowed to take the piss, or anything else you like, really. Only just arrived, mind you. Not really had chance to do more than gawp at it with a silly grin on my face.'

Jon was aware they'd gone off topic somewhat. Mind you, this was typical of Gordon, directing a conversation, steering it round until he could take control of it.

'So what can I do with my recently acquired heirloom that might satisfy the needs of our excitable young researcher, I wonder,' the assured tone indeed showing that he was directing matters.

Jon paused again. In order to ask the question, he might have to reveal something of his recent discovery. He could trust Gordon absolutely, he'd told himself. Nevertheless, this was such a momentous breakthrough, he was very reluctant to surrender ownership. Might Gordon try to take it over, he wondered. Surely not. Besides, Jon was well aware, if he wanted to make any progress, he would have to trust the man.

'It's about Alban's demise,' he began hesitantly.

'Which, oddly enough, he fails to write about in his book,' came the wry comment.

'Very droll, only, in a way, maybe he did.'

There was silence at the other end of the phone, except for the very nasal breathing. He had Gordon's attention.

'In the reports of his death –'

'Reports? There was only the one,' Gordon interrupted.

'Sorry. But you are being a pedant. One newspaper report and one written account, documented by a local magistrate who happened to be staying at the same inn, and disclosed in his notes on his death.'

'They travelled together – they weren't staying at the same inn.'

'Whatever.' Jon struggled to fight down the exasperration.

'Right. So which account are we referring to?'

It occurred to Jon that this was another way that Gordon took control – by introducing confusion while seemingly merely being precise. And it almost worked. Jon was tempted to come clean with his recent discovery. But yet he held back. He wanted to establish as many facts as he could before committing.

'The magistrate's account. He says Alban was ranting in the streets. He thought he was drunk, or however he described it –'

'Yes, 'overwhelmed by demon drink', was the expression he used,' said Gordon.

'Yes they tended not to say 'pissed as a newt' in those days, at least not in written reports by magistrates. Anyway, described him as drunk and ranting about "the Hag Witch spectre," and he should have "left her locked inside where she was found".'

'This we know. And that he was teetotal, so unlikely to be under the influence – or that particular influence. Your question – concerning the collected notes of said demised ranting madman?'

'We know he did not write of a 'hag witch' spectre, or any other witch spectre – except for the 1823 item. And that was long before he went mad – or whatever.'

'True.'

'So was there anything close – I mean, similar sounding, like 'hag' and 'witch'?'

'You mean like 'Hog Witch' or 'Hog Warts' perhaps?'

'Gordon, please, this is serious,' he had no choice but to let more out, 'Is there any place name, or house name that comes close?'

A pause. He knew that Gordon was not searching through the book, he had no need to. The man had studied it so closely he knew every page, every detail.

'You're not thinking of 'Hardwyck' I hope, because there's a few of those.'

He was fishing, and Jon knew it. What harm could it do? The name was so obscure.

'A name I've come across is … 'Haukwych'. Not seen it on any map near York that I can find. Maybe completely wrong but …'

'Hawkwych, like the bird and Wych – meaning elm?'

'N–no. Well, the 'elm' bit, yes.'

He spelt it out slowly.

'Haukwych. Hmm. Places near York, tend to end in "by" or "thorpe" of course, or "borough", "brough", "ton" – that sort of thing. An ending of "wych" doesn't seem right for that area. Mind you, we know he arrived by coach so it could be anywhere on or within reach of the route from London.'

He fell silent again and Jon pictured the man, his mind working, unravelling the mystery, assembling the pieces so they might, if not fit perfectly, have a discernible relationship. Despite the slow delivery of words, Gordon's mental acuity was phenomenal. And his capacity for retention of details was equally striking, as he demonstrated.

'There was a Haukwych I saw on an old map once. Somewhere near Northampton, Bedford, that sort of area if I recall.'

'What?' Jon could not contain his amazement – followed immediately by a sense of losing control. He'd taken a risk, revealing the name, and suddenly it seemed that he'd surrendered possession of his discovery to Gordon.

'I couldn't find anything close to that name. It ...' Jon was at a loss for words.

'So what led you to the connection, we wonder. Hag Witch to Haukwych. Bit of a leap, mind you, if you had no reference at all to a "Haukwych". Where did that come from?'

It was obvious that Jon would have to come clean. If he wanted Gordon's co-operation (and clearly he could not make any progress without it) he'd have to tell him about the letter. He took a deep breath.

'I came across a letter,' he began, then paused. 'I should be more honest with you Gordon. I've been intrigued by Alban's last days –'

'Haven't we all?'

'Indeed, and, anyway, I came across this chap, someone in the village, who deals in old correspondence, collectable stuff – you know? Like a dealer. Well I asked him to keep an eye out for anything that might mention Gerhard Alban in any way.'

'And ...?'

'Something popped up at an auction. A note really, nothing much to it.'

'And you have it?'

'Sadly, no. A Swiss dealer outbid him – it went for quite a bit in the end. Seems the postmark and stamps on the envelope were unusual. But, my chum had copied the content – and kindly passed that on.'

'It says?' Gordon was quite abrupt and Jon felt he was being reprimanded in some way for not revealing his information sooner.

'Sorry Gordon, I'll get my notebook – read it exactly.'

'This is exciting,' Gordon added, although his tone revealed no sense of that. Nevertheless, the younger man took some reassurance.

'Okay, it says: "The Rectory. Dear Alban,

A pony and trap is at your disposal and will meet you at the stage." New paragraph, "I have arranged for a workman to visit Haukwych and draw the nails in preparation as you instructed. He is an elderly man and quite deaf." new line, "I shall look forward to our meeting." Then the initials "HW" and the date "9 Oct."

'No year.'

'No, but the postmark date on the envelope was 1841.'

'And the place – postmark?'

'Bedford.'

'Hmm. Interesting indeed. So you're assuming our Alban must have been to visit a place, or house, known as Haukwych, shortly before his untimely demise. Somewhere near Bedford, we assume. That's a long way from York – and not exactly en route.'

'No, not en route, but not far off. He could have travelled to Bedford, by stage, and then on, I suppose ...' Jon let the sentence tail off, realising how feeble it must sound.

'So, I was wondering, hoping really, that Alban might have some reference to a Haukwych in the book. Maybe had recorded something he was following up on ...'

'Well, I don't hold out much hope. Anyone who'd seen a copy would have picked up on it, odd name like that.'

'Yes, I know but maybe there's something similar, you know what I mean.'

'I do. You mean "I'm stuck. I've got a damn good pointer that could lead anywhere. Can you help me please Gordon?"'

'Well, exactly.'

'I'll call you. May be a day or two, 'bye.'

Jon slowly lowered the receiver. Typical, he thought, Gordon eases into the conversation, winds you round a bit, takes over, and then "bang" – rings off and you're left wondering exactly what happened.

'Well,' he said out loud, 'This is my discovery and no-one is taking command except me!'

It had been a long and difficult journey from London to Eaton Socon, where he'd been obliged to take lodging, the coach arriving so late in the evening. It had been scheduled to arrive by two o'clock in the afternoon, or a little after, but the rutted road had caused a broken wheel somewhere between the Baldock and Biggleswade stages. By the time a repair had been effected by a local wheelwright, the journey had been delayed by some six hours. Now, there was not even the chance of hiring a local man with any sort of acceptable trap or small carriage to take him on those last few miles. Not at that time of night and with the weather so vile.

Still, the parson could wait. His first letter had stressed the urgency of an intervention, but Gerhard Alban was much experienced in these matters. If there were a presence, then it would be there the following day. Besides, a good meal should restore his demeanour. The arduous journey from London had been far from pleasant, the roads potted and muddy. The coach had barely kept to its times from the start, and the coachmen always anxious to press on, so little time was available for respite at each staging inn, even before the catastrophe. Barely sufficient time to deal with one's necessary reliefs, let alone any refreshment or chance to recover from the bruisings brought about by the lurching and jolting of the vehicle. Once they'd resumed the journey after the mishap, it was even worse. As soon as horses had been changed, the coachman was pressing the passengers to climb back in.

Alban had travelled widely in his investigations over the years but he was of mind now to limit his expeditions. There were others, younger and more resilient who could undertake these exercises. He had, to that end, arranged for a very limited and private publication of his notes. Only a handful of copies had been distributed, shared with his most trusted fellow researchers. His own copy served now as a notebook, its annotations, barely legible, light pencil markings in the margins, drafted in his own code. One day, he must set aside time to compile a cypher.

He'd been somewhat restored by the ample serving of mutton pie and potatoes, and was now finding the ale to his liking. The roaring fire had dried the muddied boots and the greatcoat, which had taken a soaking when they'd had to alight for the repair work. The landlord came to take the plate and Alban indicated that his tankard could be refilled.

'What is this place?' he called after the landlord, who paused and turned, looking puzzled.

'The name – of the inn?' continued Alban.

'Ah. You are enjoying the hospitality of the Cock Inn, at Eaton Socon,' came the reply, 'Though for how much longer we shall be able to offer it, I don't know.'

Alban tilted his head in unspoken enquiry.

'The railways, sir. The railways are coming.'

Alban nodded as the landlord went on his way. The railway. Modern travel systems sweeping away the past, delivering the future. Only, he mused, there were remnants of the past that would not be swept away, not by anything. Taking a pencil from his coat pocket, he opened his book. Finding a suitable place, he made a faint note in the central margin. He wouldn't bother to code it for now, he was too tired to concentrate and he needed better light than the guttering lamp.

It was two days before his call was returned. Jon had calmed somewhat by then, telling himself that it was unlikely that there would be any reference to Haukwych in the old book. What he'd hope for was some item somewhere about unresearched, perhaps vague, rumours or hints that could relate to that vicinity. But it would need to be vague for it not to have been followed up by anyone. In fact, he had so prepared himself that it was with a very bland tone he took the call knowing Gordon was the caller.

'Well, I did study very carefully and I can assure you –'

'Very well, thank you Gordon, and –' He hadn't been able to resist the reciprocal tease but pulled himself up short as soon as he realised how out of character it was for Gordon not to start the conversation with the usual formalities.

'Sorry! You've …' he tried to resume.

'Found nothing in print, that helps you, that is' Gordon finished for him. There was a pause.

'Come on Gordon. "In print?" What did you find?'

'Well. I don't know if this is going to help you at all but – you know that Graham got this copy from a book dealer a few years back?'

'Yes,' Jon drew out the word in anticipation.

'Well I don't think the old boy looked at it properly.'

'Really? What did you find?'

'Well, he might have done, I suppose. He did keep saying it was "a real treasure" whenever he talked to me about passing it on. Maybe he did. But why didn't he say?'

'Gordon, what is it? What did you find?'

'Well, I was searching really carefully, around that area – as you know, the book is largely geographical in structure but not totally –'

The younger man was feeling his patience strained.

'Sorry Gordon but if it's not helping me –'

'You'll want to hear this.'

'Okay?' he again drew out the word.

'I found notes.'

The hairs on the back of Jon's neck prickled.

'What sort of notes? The book is notes, essentially, in print.'

'Additional notes, in pencil – in code, mostly.'

'What? Not ...?' Jon left the question hanging.

'I reckon these are Alban's own notes, in his own code. Certain of it. So his notes, or someone who knew the code. Which is unlikely – very unlikely.'

Jon was silent, dumbfounded in fact. They knew Alban had used a code in his notes. He'd referred to it himself. The book was, in fact, the decoded notes of a lifetimes research. Alban stated in the preface that he was concerned that all he had discovered might be unavailable to others should he be 'called away' as he put it. And how prescient he had been. However, his demise two years later could hardly be described as being 'called away'.

Could Graham have obtained Alban's own copy of his printed work, and passed that on to Gordon without a hint of his knowing exactly what it was. Or maybe Gordon had guessed correctly – maybe Graham had known but chose not to say. He would have been quite elderly when he bought it. Maybe he was holding on to it while he lived, passing it on to someone younger, who might make better use of it.

'We should be able to crack the code.'

'We?'

'You've got to let me help, Gordon.' In his excitement, he'd forgotten his own investigation.

'Well, you were a little reluctant, as I recall, to let me in on your recent discovery.'

He could tell that Gordon was teasing, which made him feel even more guilty about the letter. Jon suddenly remembered.

'You said, "in code – mostly.'

'I wondered how long it would take you.' The teasing was quite obvious now.

'Come on, Gordon!'

The prickling on his neck had resumed.

'I was looking through the pages covering the Bedfordshire area and there tucked almost into the spine was this faint writing, so faint I almost missed it. It said "door" and "Cock Inn" and it could have been "e", capital e that is, and "5" or "s". So not much help to you, I'm afraid. Unless your Haukwych parson was bringing Alban to a Cock Inn somewhere."

'There could be any number of those. Are we still thinking it's the Bedford or Northampton area?'

'I checked that out. I found the map, or a scan of it. That took a while I can tell you. Anyway, there's Haukwych marked roughly between Bedford and Rushden, slightly northeast of a direct line between the two. But nothing I can see that relates to that name theses days. I'll send the scan.'

'And you checked out the Cock Inn reference, I suppose?'

'No. Only just found that. Rang you straight off.'

Jon felt guilty again. He didn't know what to say.

'Let's keep this moving, shall we?'

Jon feared again that he'd lost control but Gordon's next words reassured him.

'If you need help, let me know. You've a couple of leads to follow up on. Let's talk again when you've made progress.'

And with that, the call was terminated.

The next morning, a brighter day dawned for Alban. He breakfasted well and was outside the inn door waiting for the pony and trap that had been arranged to take him onwards.

The driver seemed a little put out, having been obliged to wait several hours the previous afternoon, but recovered when Alban made it clear he would account for the man's inconvenience with a generous fee.

It took them a good hour and a half to reach the village where the pony was changed and almost another hour, jolting along rough country lanes to reach the parsonage. So it was over an early luncheon that the anxious parson related the tale to Alban who listened so intently, he barely touched the food before him. It was agreed that he, Alban, would investigate the establishment ,commencing that very afternoon.

It was a short walk from the parsonage across flat fields to the inn. Alban and the parson walked in silence. They approached the rear of the building, an ordinary looking place, overgrown with ivy, and what might have been a large garden unkempt with almost a spinney of nondescript trees where there might have been at least grazing for pigs. The few fruit trees were spilling their rotting produce amongst the thistles and other weeds. The two stopped at the edge of the field that bounded the garden and the parson handed the key to Alban. The latter nodded in acknowledgment and without a word, the grim-faced parson turned and, as arranged, left Alban to his investigations.

After he had twice circumnavigated the building, once at a fair distance to get a feel for the setting, then at close quarters, Alban set about entering the premises. There were three doors, one at the back which probably led into some sort of kitchen, another set to one side of the front elevation, the third was the main door. That is, it must have been the main entrance at some time but was clearly disused, its shabby condition noticeably worse than the state of the remainder of the inn. Even so, the door had something about it, a solidity that was ill-fitting with the surrounding dilapidation. Alban eyed the large key, then selected a slightly smaller one and with that unlocked the second front door and pushed it open. Instinctively, Alban drew his greatcoat closer round him, took up his bag and stepped inside.

The evening was drawing in, though there was still light enough. There were candles, or what was left of them, on one or two of the tables. Alban opened his bag and extracted a friction light, using it to ignite one of the candle stubs. The stuttering light illuminated more of the room and Alban moved to a second table, igniting a second candle. There was now sufficient light to illuminate the heavy curtain that hung over the larger door. He did not approach it immediately but that was the focus of his attention as he moved around the interior of the inn.

Once the room was fully illuminated, Alban set his bag on one of the tables and began to take in the layout of the place. It was not big, being a typical small country inn. A main room with small windows looking to the front and to one side, a small serving counter at the side of which stood a doorway. Investigation revealed this to lead to what must be a dining area, and a further door opened into a humble kitchen with an external door opening onto a yard. Through a third door in the dining area was a staircase leading to the upper floor. Alban swiftly ascertained that, as had been agreed, but for himself, the building was deserted. In fact, from what the parson had told him, there was not the remotest chance that it would be otherwise.

Alban cleared a table in the main room close to the heavy curtain and placed his bag on it. He took a large hammer and crowbar from the bag and carefully pulled back the stained curtain, coughing as clouds of dust fell from its folds even though they had very recently been disturbed. The revealed door was as had been described, solidly made and heavily barred. Strong planks had been nailed across, as if to withstand some mighty onslaught from outside. Alban allowed himself a grim smile, acknowledging the futility of the physical bracing against an otherworldly intrusion. He glanced once around the room then set about removing the already loosened nails, propping the heavy planks carefully against the wall to one side of the door.

Pulling away the last of the planks, Alban noticed a distinct change in the atmosphere of the room. It was as if he had opened the door itself and let in colder air to the already chill room. A quick look at the candles showed, as he suspected, no draughts and the door was still secured shut by heavy bolts, top and bottom. Furthermore, he was becoming aware of an aroma, unusual although not unknown to him. At first he struggled to distinguish this scent from the ambient smell of the inn itself, the noticeable stench of sour ale and stale tobacco smoke, both of which he abhorred – fresh or stale. It gradually became clearer to him. It was a subtle but quite distinctive smell, one not easily described being at once sour, musty, slightly sweet and sickening. It caught the back of his throat and he tried hard not to breathe deeply. It was what one might expect to find, after some considerable time had passed, in a coffin, or other confined space that held some human remains, yet more ancient than the smell of mere decay.

It took Jon just 24 hours to complete his enquiries. Even he was astonished by how easily things fell into place. Now, he felt, he could share a little more with his mentor. He dialled the number. This time there was no interruption of answering device.

'Young man,' came the immediate response.

'I've found the Cock Inn, I'm pretty sure.'

'Brilliant, where?'

'Eaton Socon. But, not there anymore. Doesn't exist, the inn, that is.'

'I guessed you didn't mean the town. Well done. So trail ends there? You don't sound disappointed to me.'

'No trail starts there. Well, it did for Alban. Sort of.'

'Calm down, my boy, and let's get things straight.'

Jon relaxed. He was again feeling a real excitement of anticipation.

'Okay. The Cock Inn referred was, as I said, in Eaton Socon – hence the ES. It was a coaching inn, a stage on the London to York route until the 1840s when it became a private house. So I believe that was where Alban left the stage coach and went on by pony and trap, as detailed in the note.'

'The reference to "door"?'

'Could just be where he was to meet the driver, the pony and trap. He didn't code it so ...'

'Right. And Haukwych?'

'Well, your scan of the old map gave a rough location, and using other mapping, old Ordnance Survey and whatever, I found a hamlet, unnamed, a few miles north of Bedford – about a pony and trap distance from Eaton Socon, I'd say. About ten miles by country lanes.'

'Still there?'

'No.'

'Ah.'

'Not the hamlet. But there is an old inn, closed now. And it is called 'The Falcon!'

'So?'

'Falcon – Hawk. Previously been called the Falconer's Arms, and the Hand in Glove.'

'Bit tenuous – Haukwych, Hawk, Falcon, don't you think.'

'Maybe but – there's history.'

'Go on,'

'The pub's closed now, as I said. Never been much of a success – the place, as far as I can gather. Not as a pub. Was a private house for a while in the 1930s but ...'

It was all coming out in a rush.

'But what?'

'The owners upped and left. Overnight – virtually. Went to Australia.'

'Really!'

Jon could feel the surging interest.

'Track 'em down?'

'Died – childless. And reclusive.'

'And had they ...'

'They had been outgoing, by all accounts, before they left. Well, one or two accounts. He ran a business in the area – to do with agricultural equipment, employed quite a few people, often threw parties, firm's outings – and they were usually the life and soul of anything, it seems.'

'So that's what caught your eye, eh? And, we think – you think – something must have happened. Something life-changing. Interesting. The building?'

'Old, eighteenth century. Probably built as an inn. Or a farmhouse that became one..'

'Mind you, I still say, it is a long way from Bedford to York.'

'He probably took the coach up from Eaton Socon, or another stage, to York. Of course he'd have to get to the Great North Road. Probably took the pony and trap. Why wouldn't he?' he paused, reckoning that Gordon, by saying little, might be thinking along the same lines. Jon went on.

'I believe something phenomenal might have happened. He must have – could have been investigating the inn.'

'Must have?' Gordon was fishing again but Jon had nothing more that he hadn't shared.

'I reckon it's possible, why not?'

He didn't add that he believed Alban might have travelled to York to get away as far as possible, and might have been hoping to travel further when he collapsed and then died, although he'd already convinced himself of it.

'So, no actual mention of occurrences there?'

Jon saw now how unconvincing his theory could seem.

'Now, in the note – to Alban – the parson says he's had the nails drawn. And by a man who's deaf. What do we make of that, young Jon?'

'Floorboards, possibly? Or a door? Hence the reference in Alban's notes.'

'Maybe. Intriguing, I do admit. So, what's your next move?'

The question rather caught Jon by surprise. His mind had wandered from the phone call.

'This is my next move,' he replied, rather warily. He wondered if, despite his reassurances, Gordon might want to get more involved. And Gordon involved invariably meant Gordon running the show.

'Well, I'd want to take a closer look, of course.'

'You say the establishment is closed.'

'Closed and on offer as a 'business investment'.'

' Do you think that could be because ...?'

'No. I think it's probably the wrong business in the wrong place – being a pub in that location. Simple as that. Wouldn't work as a coaching inn – it's not near enough the Bedford to Wellingborough road. Nowadays, with drink-driving laws, no-one would be driving there. Not much local trade as it's too far from nearest villages, which have their own pubs. Last landlord drank too much – probably because no-one else was drinking anything there. No record of sightings, or sensations, that I can find. Besides, we would have heard about it, wouldn't we? There would have been a hint or whisper someone would have picked up. However ...,' he left it hanging.

'There's more.'

'Well this is also tenuous but I think it stacks up. The parson – HW.'

'Found him?'

'No. Well, not there. What I found was a Reverend Herbert Wedgewood of Bedford on the passenger list of a ship bound for South Africa in 1844 but ...'

'Yes?'

'Vanished – in transit. Believed to have been lost overboard.

As I say, it's all tenuous, Gordon, but ...'

'Aren't the best ones always that way?' the older man finished for him. He was silent for a moment.

'We wonder if the parson was touched by, er, whatever. Hmm,' he paused, 'So what's your plan, young Jonathan? I do expect you have a plan.'

'I am going to have a look. I've arranged it.'

In fact he hadn't, but he wanted Gordon to think he was further ahead, just in case the older man was thinking of insinuating himself to a greater degree in the investigation than Jon would like. He desperately wanted to control this himself. He knew how big it could be – to discover the very place that had driven the most celebrated ghost seeker completely mad. Maybe to find the actual phenomenon.

'Pretending to be a potential investor, I suppose. Wear your slickest suit.'

'No. It's been on the market for some time. I've told the agents I'm a film maker – which I am – and think it could make a good set for a production. If it's OK – that is, if I get a feel that it deserves further investigation – we would rent it for a few weeks. We'd get permission to do some cosmetic changes – so we could poke about. And see what we find.'

'Who's a clever boy?'

'If the hip's up to it, you could come and check it out. We'd be able to find a beer somewhere, I expect.'

'But not there,' Gordon chuckled.

'No, I doubt the beer's ever been good there.'

'Keep me informed of progress. Cheers.'

Alban stepped back from the door. He reached into his bag and took out a small flask. He took a sip then held the open flask to his nose, as if flushing his nostrils with a disinfecting, countering smell. Replacing the flask in the bag, he again drew the collar of his coat close around his neck. He wondered if even he dare to actually open the door. He drew breath and stepped forward. The large key turned the lock surprisingly easily but it took more than a few moments to loosen and withdraw the stubborn bolts from their staples. Having succeeded, he decided another reinforcing nip of brandy would be sensible. There was now a very noticeable chill, far greater than would be found in an empty house for the time of year. Alban noticed with some surprise that his hand trembled as he uncorked the flask. His legs, too, were not steady and he thought to sit awhile before opening the door. He was determined that he must do so but not immediately. He took his book from the pocket of the coat, found the pencil and would have written a note or two, recording his actions so far but then replaced both items and sat back.

Anyone passing at that moment would have been astonished and alarmed by what happened next. They would have witnessed a man emerge quite suddenly from the small door at the front of the darkened building, flailing his arms about most violently and screaming, screaming like a madman. The fellow ran one way, then turned and ran the other, all the while flailing as if fighting off a swarm of bees, or vicious bats, although nothing could be seen resembling either. The screaming was incessant and pitiful as the man made off down the road running far faster than would have been expected for someone of his build.

Behind him, the faint light that barely illuminated the doorway, flickered and failed as the candles within were extinguished, perhaps by a draught from the open door, thought the night was still. Still as a grave.

Eventually, clearly exhausted by his exertions Alban's pace slowed a little yet he did not stop. He dare not. He no longer waved his arms about but now and again would half turn, as if to see if he was pursued, then would turn back and quicken his pace. By then the screaming had quieted to a wailing or moaning. This finally faded to a pitiful whimpering as the wretched man stumbled onwards.

There was a small car parking area in front of the drab looking building and barely legible sign indicating further parking to the rear. Jon parked in front and strolled around to the rear to get a look at the building. He had not known what to expect. The few images he'd found in his research were mostly old views. Even online mapping and satellite views were indistinct, images taken on a day of poor visibility he supposed.

The toot of a horn caught his attention and he returned to see another car parked beside his. A smartly dressed young lady emerged from the driver's door.

'Mr Spelling?'

He smiled in confirmation.

'I have the keys here. Do you mind awfully showing yourself around? I'll let you in, of course.'

'No, that's fine. I'd be happy to explore on my own.'

'Only, well it smells a bit, you know, musty, or something, and I've got a meeting later that ... And we do have all your details, so ...'

'That's absolutely fine,' Jon assured her, "couldn't be better" he was thinking, although he couldn't help wondering what the 'smell' might actually be. Could she be unknowingly sensitive to spectral activity?

She stepped towards the door. Jon had already noted that it was quite modern looking wooden door. A small porch stood forward from the main wall. To the left, a single storey, box-like structure evidenced the addition of a room to the front of the original building. The agent unlocked the outer door and handed Jon the keys.

'Could you drop them back at the office when you've done, please?'

She seemed in a hurry to get away, or was Jon imagining that, he wondered. However, before she reached her car, she turned.

'I meant to ask, what sort of film is it?'

Jon was caught off-guard for a moment.

'You said it was for a film location.'

'Of course. Um, not allowed to say. Sorry. Not yet. If it goes ahead, there would need to be non-disclosure agreements. You know. Some major players, stars needing no publicity. I mean, for the time being, you understand.'

It sounded rather lame but he hoped it would be enough to satisfy her curiosity.

'Wow!" she said, 'Of course. Hope it suits your needs. Might give it the much-needed boost to its sales potential.'

She glanced once more at the building, pulled a face, then smiled at Jon as she climbed into the car.

She was quite attractive, Jon reflected as she drove away. But far more attractive was the prospect before him. He pushed open the outer door and went into the porch.

Jon was not surprised to find the inner door, leading from the porch into the main bar area, to be a modern construction, like its outer counterpart. Glazed panels, each pane with a variety of faded and peeling stickers displaying the usual warnings, prohibitions, claims to qualifications and promoted items. He was not at all dismayed. If it was indeed a door he was seeking, it was unlikely to be a door that was well-used. Much more likely to be some small closet door, or a trap-door in one of the floors.

He paused and sniffed at the air. There was a distinctly musty smell to the place, as might be expected in a closed-up pub, no matter how little used. But it was nothing out of the ordinary as far as he could tell.

The windows were not curtained, only the dirt on the glass dimming the daylight but leaving sufficient to illuminate the room. This was quite large, filling the width of the building. What must be a boxed-in central beam showed how the room might have at some time been divided. At the further end of the room, away from the entrance was an entryway in the wall. It led through to a separate area, presumably a dining room, added to the front of the original building. Jon recalled how ugly this structure was from the outside and it was equally unattractive within.

He took a half hour or so to explore the rest of the building, screwing his face up at the general appearance. He tried to imagine how it might have looked in Alban's time, without the very basic additions. Mostly consisting of shoddily installed boxing, like that on the ceiling of the main bar, these presumably covered period features. A short corridor, accessed from the lounge bar, led to a small toilet area, made with flimsy partitions providing for lady customers' needs. At the end of the corridor was a door marked 'Gents' which clearly led to the small outhouse extension he had seen in the carpark. This also had an outer door but he estimated the extension must have been constructed in the late twentieth centruy, so was of no interest to him.

In fact, there were no obvious doors to capture his imagination, neither on the ground floor or amongst the first floor rooms. A simple loft hatch from the upstairs landing easily lifted but nothing seemed in any way odd. There was a trapdoor behind the bar which was also easily lifted, revealing steps, constructed in fairly recent years, leading down to the cellar. This turned out to be a small, cramped space, hung with cobwebs and reeking of stale beer. It ran from beneath the bar itself to what he estimated was the back of the building. A hatch at the rear indicated the access for bringing in barrels. He decided he would give the cellar some more detailed attention later.

Returning to the ground floor, it occurred to him that perhaps the cellar had been purposely reduced in size. Why wouldn't it fill the full width of the building? He began to stamp on the carpeted floor, hoping perhaps to discover some trapdoor other than the one behind the bar.

The sudden ringing of his mobile telephone startled him. He saw it was Gordon calling and inwardly groaned.

'Gordon, how are you?'

'Are you in?'

'Yes. Been here an hour or so. Just getting the lie of the place. Run down and shabby describes it best. No wonder no-one ever came here.'

'Listen, I'm a getting a funny feeling about this.'

'You're picking that up over the phone? I'm impressed. Wonder of modern technology, eh?'

'I'm serious. I had a really good look though Alban's notes. I found the word "door" pencilled in again – several times.'

'Really? I thought you'd looked.'

'I had. But I'd concentrated on pages covering that area, near Bedford. These were elsewhere in the book, all faint, sometimes a bit wobbly, the writing, but quite clearly "door".'

'Fascinating. Maybe written while travelling? Hence the wobbly writing?'

'Or as his mind was steadily disintegrating, as it seems it must have been. I'm not sure you should go on with this, not on your own.'

Up to this point, the hair on the back of Jon's neck had been prickling with this new reference. So, it was a door he would be looking for. He tried to picture where it might be, what it might look like. But the 'not on your own' bit snapped him back to the call. Typical Gordon, trying to muscle in, maybe take over.

'Hold on, Gordon. Nothing to get alarmed about. I'm not getting much feedback here. There may be nothing at all. After all, we're still not certain this is the place. We could be miles off –'

He stopped abruptly. The entrance – it was in the wrong

place. A building like this would have the door bang in the centre of the front wall. He looked across to the dining section. This would be a later addition, breaking out through the front wall.

'Jon, are you there?'

'Hold on Gordon, I just want to try something.'

He approached the wall between the bar and the dining area. Glancing each way, he estimated where the centre of the room must be. Warily, he stepped forward and began to knock on the wall, first moving one way along the wall, then the other. There was a stretch of wall that sounded hollow. It could have been merely architectural convenience when the extension was added yet, he wondered, why bury a door?

'Jon?'

'I'll call you back, Gordon. I'll let you know how I get on.'

He rang off and even as he did so, he became aware of an odd smell. An unpleasant, unsettling smell, barely detectable but definitely present.

He had not come prepared. He had agreed to look around today, assess whether the building warranted further exploration. If so, he would officially 'rent' it for the supposed film shoot. Then he could take time to dig deeper, perhaps literally. But this could not wait. He could deal with permissions and paperwork later. He had to know if the wall hid a door. And if it did, was that door special in some way.

Jon stripped off his jacket. He'd seen some tools in the cellar – a spade and a screwdriver. There should probably be a mallet too. He was right. Gathering these he hurried back to the lounge. There was little in the way of furniture so clearing a work area was simple. He took a look at the other side of the wall – what would have been outside in Alban's time. Though there was little activity on the road, he'd heard barely a couple of vehicles passing during the time he'd been there, he recalled, he thought it better to tackle the partition from the lounge.

He took a massive swing at the wall with the edge of the spade, using it more as an axe. The first blow pierced the plasterboard. Encouraged by this he took several more swings before pausing to pull away the broken fragments. The hole he'd cleared was still small. There was not enough light to show anything within.

A few more blows and, using the spade as a lever, he managed to clear a good area. Immediately beneath the plasterboard, there was a wooden frame, the stud structure supporting the wall. The light was dimming in the pub but there was still sufficient to show the edge of a heavy door frame. The stud-work was secured to the edge of the frame. He realised he was not in the middle but to one side of the door. He'd expected it to be wider.

Spurred on, Jon was determined now to remove as much of the plasterboard as he could. If he wanted to free up the stud-work, he would need a claw-hammer or a wrecking bar. He was thinking about this as he swung and levered the fragments of plasterboard. He cursed himself for not having the foresight to come equipped. Surely, a pub would have such a thing as claw-hammer. Why wouldn't they, he wondered.

It was now getting quite dark. Jon paused. He needed to think. Work out what the best plan was. Maybe not hand back the keys, not tonight. Drive home, get tools, come back in the morning, early. But that was time lost. He recalled he had an electric tyre pump in the car – and it had a lamp. He raced outside and retrieved the pump. He was delighted to see how bright the LED lamp was. Back in the pub, he checked the cellar again, forcing himself to take the time to search carefully. And there was a very rusted, but still useful claw-hammer. Gathering it, he thought to look in one of the open wall cupboards. They'd seemed empty but in one he found a box of candles, useful sized ones, he gratefully acknowledged, not the tea lights that might have been. Maybe they had been prepared for power-cuts. More likely, for disconnection of power through not paying bills, he mused as he quickly made his way back to the lounge. Then he recalled he didn't have matches. How could he light the candles? A swift rummage amongst the abandoned debris behind the bar and his prayers were answered. A match-book with just six remaining unused cardboard matches.

He paused to draw breath. He lit one of the candles and placed it carefully so that it cast enough light to illuminate his immediate work area. Just one energetic swing of the spade extinguished the flame. He dared not use the lamp, fearing the battery would run out before he'd finished. He swore. A moment later, he was back behind the bar. There were no pint mugs, which he'd thought would make an ideal candle holder, sheltering the flame. Tucked under the sink he found one grubby bottle of clear glass. He gave it just a moment's thought then wrapped the bottle in his jacket and smashed the neck with the hammer. With the neck removed he was able to set a candle into the base of the bottle. He caught his hand on the jagged glass but barely paused to wipe the blood. The urgency was too great. He had to reveal the door.

The improvised candle holder worked perfectly. Soon he

was back at the demolition site and within half an hour, he'd cleared the plasterboard over the door area. He paused briefly, breathing heavily. Holding the bottle up, he could clearly see the dark, peeling paintwork on the heavy door. And he could see the heavy battens of wood that were nailed across it. His eyes gleamed with satisfaction. Had he made the greatest discovery of all, he wondered. Wouldn't his name go down in history if this was indeed the door that had brought about the end of the great Gerhard Alban? His phone rang, startling him.

'Gordon. What can I do for you?'

'I'm worried, old man. Are you still there, at the place?'

'No. Just got home. Left there a while ago. It was getting dark and I could barely see anything. No power.'

He turned to the windows and saw it was indeed dark. So some of what he was saying was true.

'Look, I don't want to get involved, well, that's clearly not true. I do want to be involved, I don't want to take over. It's your find, and I'm fine with that, but I am worried. I've been thinking about it, and if it did for Alban, this is serious. You shouldn't be alone, I mean, when you're poking about there. When are you going back?'

'Oh, probably tomorrow, I should think. Not sure it's leading anywhere, to be honest.'

He'd never lied like this to Gordon, or to anyone. Well, he might have exaggerated a client pitch occasionally, but in this work, he'd always been completely, or nearly completely honest. Pinocchio came to mind and he almost laughed out loud.

'Let me come over, to your place, tomorrow. I'm back

driving now. Let's chat about best approach, eh? Risk assessment stuff, you know?'

'Of course, Gordon. Great idea. Much appreciated. Er, ring before you set off, eh?'

Jon wanted to get the older man off the line, get on with the demolition. He reckoned he could have it clear in an hour. Then tackle the other side. He turned the phone off, not waiting for any response. Too anxious to continue. For a fleeting moment, rationality tugged at his conscience. He dismissed it. Now for the claw-hammer, he decided.

———

It was the parson, the following morning, who found the bag in the abandoned inn. And he who locked, re-bolted and nailed up the door, drawing the curtain across to conceal it, all the time in silent but urgent prayer. He took the bag back to the parsonage but did not hear from Gerhard Alban ever again. He was not greatly surprised. His mind was made up. This was too much for him. Perhaps in his younger days, the vigour of his piety would have given him the strength to deal with the matter. Now, at his time of life, he would be best putting as much distance as he could between himself and that hellish place. He'd heard there was need of men of the cloth in the new provinces in Africa. Perhaps that, he decided, could be his last calling.

———

A wild energy drove Jon onwards in his task. He had no

thought of hunger or thirst, nor of injury, and there were several, fortunately minor. Or perhaps not so fortunately in the circumstances. A more major wound, or damage to a limb, might have stopped him. But he seemed possessed, a driven man.

He cleared the stud-work from the inside of the door-frame surprisingly easily. It occurred to him that it must have been installed in a hurry. Encouraged by this, he was about to tackle the planks that barred the door itself but thought better of it. Gathering his implements and the candle, he went though to the dining room, carefully paced the wall to measure the position of the door, and immediately set about the further side. This also took an hour or so to remove to the same degree as the first side. He forced himself to take time as he worked to clear away the debris, not for the sake of tidiness but only to remove any hazard that might slow his progress. There were no bars across the door on its outer side, he discovered.

Satisfied with all he'd accomplished, he returned to the barred inside of the door. Testing the topmost of the four battens, he was pleased to find it gave a little as he tugged at one end of it. Thrusting the plank back, there was enough of the roughly made brad nails to get a purchase with the claw hammer. They pulled easily. With one end of the plan free, he could lever the other end and draw the nails from there. In a similar way, he removed the lowest batten, then the third. The last plank was the stoutest and he wondered if this too would pull with ease, or perhaps would offer some resistance. He realised he'd come to regard the door itself as a restrained malevolent being, some sort of malevolent entity contained by these rough planks. He wiped his mouth with the back of his hand, aware of how dry he was. It was then he noticed the dank, foul aroma had increased. It was not yet overpowering but it was enough for him to lift his arm to cover his nose. A moment later, the whole building was plunged into darkness.

A stifled cry escaped him before he realised he'd not attended to the candle. He'd replaced it only once in all this time and in his excitement, he'd forgotten to monitor. He could smell the extinguished wick and paused a moment wondering if this in fact had been the source of the foulish odour. Leaning forward towards the door, he confirmed that it was not. Cursing, he groped his way over to the small table that held the makeshift candle holder. He could not find the match-book. He fought down the sense of panic that began to arise.

'Calm,' he told himself out loud, 'Just stay calm. The lamp!'

Moving his foot about, he was able to locate the pump and reaching down he fumbled for the switch. The light immediately came on. Clutching the lamp, he swung it round to light up the old door. It looked exactly as it had earlier only now more brightly lit.

'Idiot,' he told himself, as if in reprimand.

He found a replacement candle and managed to set it in the soft wax of its predecessor. As he lit with one of the remaining matches, he saw that his hand was shaking. Maybe he should have waited, taken up Gordon's offer. Maybe this was too dangerous for one person.

'Don't be stupid. Idiot! Idiot! Idiot! Come on, man. We can do this!'

He was hugging himself, willing himself on, acting as if he was a team of several, not a lone individual. Emboldened by his own rhetoric, he turned off the lamp. The candle itself seemed to falter, sputtering in its glass casing. He wondered if it might be faulty in some way, perhaps he should replace it, or have a second one lit. As he was not expecting now to be so vigorous in his exertions, it would not need any container. Decision made, he took another of the candles and, having lighted it from the first, he placed it on the floor to the left side of the doorway.

Now he was ready to remove the last of the securing battens.

This proved harder than the others. Not only was it a heavier plank of wood but it seemed far more securely fixed. It took all his strength, using the spade as a lever, to pull it forward from its fixing. But it finally loosened just enough to let him draw the brads. These were much bigger, fashioned no doubt in some local blacksmith's shop. He imagined someone asking for the stoutest nails that could be made and driven. He paused briefly to take breath and recover his strength, and only then wondered how such a thought came to him.

Taking a grip of the loosened end of the batten and placing his foot against the ancient door frame, he gave an almighty heave. To his relief, the other end gave, much more easily. He briefly considered that perhaps he should have started with that end. But there was no time for such pointless contemplation. It was loose enough and he wrestled and tore at the piece until it too came free.

He staggered back with the beam then placed it carefully on the floor away from the door. Taking up the crude candle holder, he stepped forward to examine the door itself. Massive bolts secured it top and bottom. They were fitted vertically to secure above the door and into the floor at the base. He wondered if they would yield, not having been opened for so many, many years. Then he saw the lock. It was the size of a church door lock. It would need a suitably sized key – and he did not recall there being any substantial key on the set he'd been given. Why would there be? Who would need a key to a door that was, to all intents and purposes, not there? He struck his head with the heel of his hand in frustration. Now what?

––––––––––––––

How Alban found his way to Eaton Socon and the Cock Inn nobody would know. He certainly could not have said. It was early afternoon when he stumbled up the street. The coach was standing by waiting for the last passengers to climb in. Seeing it, Alban quickened his pace. He called to the coachman.

'Wait! I pray you wait!'

There was some confusion. Here was a dishevelled man, mud-spattered and clearly in a state of agitation. The coachman called down to the ostler, asking if he knew the man. Perhaps he was a wandering vagrant.

'I have money. I have a ticket. Are you London bound?'

'This is the York coach, fellow,' called out the coachman. You'll need to –'

But the old man interrupted him.

'York! Good. I have a ticket, see.'

The coachman secured the reigns and climbed down and indeed the man did have a ticket, issued for the Royal Express just a few days previously, and still valid for travel. The ostler looked at the coachman who shrugged.

'Do you have luggage?' he asked.

The old man looked nonplussed. He had no bag at all, just a book clutched tightly in his hand.

'No. No luggage,' He seemed to be puzzled himself. 'It was sent on, yes, sent on.' He added lamely.

The old man turned now and again and looked back the way he'd come, as if someone might come after him. The coachman wondered then, pulling a face, acknowledged that the ticket was acceptable. The man sounded like a gentleman, despite his appearance.

'There's no room within,' he said, then called up, 'Make room for one more on top.'

By the time the coach reached Newark late that evening, there were just two other passengers and therefore room enough for Alban to sit within the coach. It was here that a magistrate joined the travellers. He, too, took his place inside the carriage. It was not long after the coach departed that he became aware of the muttering of one his fellow passengers.

At the next, and the following stages, when they alighted to stretch aching limbs, this odd man kept himself to himself. His coat was mud-stained, the magistrate noted, and the man would, from time to time when there was illumination enough, write, or at least attempt to write in a book he carried. The odd thing was, he wrote with his pencil in the tight margin of the binding. Surely it would be easier to make notes in the outer margin, even for the very short jottings the man made.

———————

There was nothing else for it, Jon decided, than to break

the lock off. It was a huge contraption mounted on the one side of the door. It looked to be made of wood with metal reinforcings. He set the edge of the spade at the top of the lock and used it as a sort of chisel, driving it down with blows from the hammer. The clang as he struck at it made his own ears ring. It took a good dozen blows before he had sufficient purchase behind the lock to haul on it. The lock splintered and cracked and then came loose enough for him to disengage the thick metal tongue from the keep in the door frame.

Now for the bolts. Again, Jon noticed the shaking of his hands. Surely, he thought, the result of all this physical exertion. Just not used to it, he chided himself, must get to the gym, get in shape for things like this.

'Things like what exactly?', he wondered. This was altogether new territory for him. He took a breath then grasped the handle at the end of the top bolt. He tested it with a little concerted pull. Nothing moved. Taking another breath, he pulled harder. Still nothing. He gave himself a moment, then hauled as hard as he could, using all his weight. The bolt moved slightly, then with a groaning sound of metal scraping against metal, the bolt shifted. A second pull brought it clear of its securing staple. He pushed gingerly at the body of door. It was unyielding. He would need to release the bottom bolt before trying it properly. He glanced round at the candles. Neither seemed to have burnt down much. He must be making good progress, he noted. The lower bolt felt just as secure as its partner. He wondered how much force he could muster. He couldn't use his weight so it would be muscle power alone. Bracing himself, he took hold of the handle and hauled upwards. He feared it might be too much for his back – and again wished he'd kept himself fitter – but after a moment or two he felt it give slightly. Relaxing for a moment, he once again hauled with all his strength and finally, with a similar sound of metal scraping against metal, it too yielded to his efforts and drew clear of the hole in the stone floor that had secured it.

Jon stepped back breathing heavily. He leaned on the table for a moment, flexing his hands to restore the blood flow. His muscles ached but he had such a sense of achievement. Wait till he told Gordon about this. He realised for the first time that he had completely forgotten to take notes. He should have recorded every moment, every action. This would be unforgivable. He cast about him, searching for his jacket with the notebook in the pocket. Maybe he should take time now to record events, try to recall everything, the odour, the location of the door, the … . He realised he was struggling to recall everything that had occurred. He'd been acting like a madman, just tearing away without any thought for serious research. He stepped away towards the bar recalling that was where he last had the jacket, he thought.

Then he heard the knocking. Jon swung round. He looked over at the entrance door to the pub, wondering if it could be from there, though he knew it wasn't. It had come from the old door. His mouth was dry and his hands shook. Even his legs felt unsteady. Nevertheless he threw himself across the room and round into the dining area, scared at what he might see yet too afraid to stay where he was. There was nothing. Even in the dim light cast by the candle from the table in the adjoining lounge, he could see there was nothing. The knocking sounded again, lightly but distinctly – a knocking on the ancient door.

Jon was paralysed. What had he done? What unworldly being might he have released?

Suddenly he heard a voice, a female voice, faltering but clear and in the other room.

'Who's there? Who ... who's there?'

Jon felt a wave of relief. Someone must have come in, wondering what was going on, perhaps she'd seen the flickering candle.

He raced back round the partition – but there was no-one.

He couldn't have imagined it, surely. It had been so clear. Then he heard her again.

'Who's there?'

The voice was close beside his ear. He gasped and fell back, striking the table. He stared wildly about him. How was this happening? It must be some trick, surely.

'Who's there?' she said again, this time beside his other ear. He instinctively waved his arm as if to swat away the voice.

'Who's there?'

Again, only it was no longer faltering, nor gentle. There was scornful laughter in it, 'Who's there?'

It was round his head, so close, and the stench was unbearable. Jon could barely breathe.

'Who's there? Who's there?' It was incessant, and so insistent. It seemed to get even closer, to be almost inside his head.

Jon screamed. He waved his arms about trying to drive the thing off. He had to get out, get away. He rushed for the entrance door, colliding again with the table as he went. Thankfully he'd left the door unlocked but even outside, the voice continued. He stared wildly about him, all the time frantically thrashing at the endlessly tormenting voice.

'Who's there? Who's there?'

'Leave me alone!' Jon screamed. He looked around helplessly, desperate to get away. There was utter darkness and he knew he needed light.

He started to run into the darkness, stumbling as he went. He lost his footing and fell to his knees. Still the voice persisted. Suddenly he became aware of light – his only hope. The light grew stronger. He scrambled to his feet and ran desperately towards it, arms flailing until the light was upon him. He fell gratefully before it.

———————

The coach pulled into the yard of York's White Swan early the following morning. It had made good time, despite the weather, and the passengers were thankful for that at least, as they gingerly extricated themselves from on top and inside the wagon. Seeing him now clearly in daylight, the magistrate regarded the strange passenger with some curiosity. The man still clutched his book while looking about him as if confused as to his whereabouts, or as if seeking some person who might greet his arrival. Taking it on himself to see if he might assist, he approached the old man and asked if he was to be met. The man seemed taken aback, fearful almost, again and again he twisted his head round, seeming to seek out someone. But all he would say was 'hog witch' but in such a low whisper, the magistrate could barely make it out. He could see that the man was dressed in good clothes, although they were torn and muddied. He was clearly a man of some standing, it would seem. Being unable to offer any useful service, he bid the old man farewell and set off with his own bag to his city home. 'Hog witch', he wondered, or was it 'hag witch'? Clearly this old man was troubled in his mind.

Several hours later, the magistrate chanced again upon the man not far from where he had left him. But now the fellow seemed even more agitated. He waved his book about above his head as if beating at flies, though at that time of year there clearly were none. He was ranting, babbling in Latin and in other languages. Around him, young children gawped and grinned, others laughed out loud. The magistrate approached one man and asked what was going on.

'T'old gaffers off 'is head,' came the reply, 'Drunk as a lord, I'd say,' said the man with a laugh.

At that moment, the old man set off at a pace away down the street. Reaching the corner, to the delight of his now substantial audience, he peered round it then raced back. He stopped abruptly when he saw the magistrate, clearly recognising him. The latter was astonished, and considerably embarrassed. A moment later, the old man proffered the book he had so carefully cherished. The magistrate took it and the old man hoarsely whispered to him. Then suddenly collapsed, falling against the wall of the building beside which they stood.

'Hog witch?' the magistrate asked, 'What of this "hog witch"?'

But his question was unheard by Gerhard Alban, for he had expired, free at last from his tormentor.

'He came out of nowhere,' said the truck driver, 'waving his arms about. Suddenly ran straight at me. I slammed on the breaks but I was on top of him almost the moment I saw him,' he paused, 'Honestly.'

'It's alright,' the police officer reassured him. 'Breathalyser's negative. You're in shock. We can take a statement later. Just drink your tea.'

The driver was still white as a sheet, clearly distressed by the accident. But he obviously wanted to talk about it.

'Weirdest thing was, by the time I'd pulled up, I went back, and there's no-one about. He's just lying there in a terrible state. I could see he was finished, there was nothing I could do. I knelt down and then, I looked up, you know, hoping someone, a car or another truck, anything, would come. But it's a quiet road, that's why I use it. Anyway, I looked up, and there's this woman just standing there, looking at him. I said "call the police, call an ambulance!" and she just looked at him – she was smiling. Then she'd gone, when I looked up again. I looked round and she was going into the pub. That old pub's been shut for ages. She went in and I could see it was on fire. The whole pub flames coming out of everywhere, and she just seemed to walk into it, calm as anything. I didn't know what to do. By the time I'd rung 999 and you lot and the fire people turned out, the pub was completely ablaze, like a massive bonfire, it was. It was like a weird dream, a nightmare – just happening around me.'

Gordon and Arthur sat in silence. Before them on Gordon's

desk lay Alban's book.

'I can't believe it,' Gordon was saying, 'He told me he'd gone home, was going back in the morning. I offered to go with him. You know, go as backup. No-one should tackle something like that on their own. You wouldn't, would you?'

'Of course not. It's not your fault, Gordon. How could you have known? He was young.'

'Yes, he was young. Too young. I should never have encouraged him. Honestly, I didn't think there was anything in it, to be honest. Just these vague jottings. Nothing else to go on, no sound evidence. I was just, I don't know, letting him have his head.'

'But you did wonder, surely, didn't you? I mean, if there was something more. Why did you offer to go over.?'

'I don't know, Arthur. Yes, when I looked through the book, I found the notes. I kept missing them, then finding more. It gave me an odd feeling.'

'Well, we'll never know now. Place was burned to the ground, totally destroyed. If it was a door, as you, or as Jon thought, it's not there now. Whatever presence was there will have gone with it. '

'True. Unless there was something left over. It would have to be something that had been there before, when there was a visitation. That could have carried some contamination, if there was anything.'

Gordon looked down at the book and said 'Oh Christ!'.

BIBLIOGRAPHY

Green, A. (1974 edition) *Our Haunted Kingdom*
Fontana/Collins
Jones, Richard (2004) *Haunted Inns of Britain & Ireland*
New Holland
King, William H. (2005) *Haunted Bedfordshire: A Ghostly Compendium* The Book Castle
King, William H. (2012) *Haunted Bedford*
The History Press – Kindle edition
Mackay, Anthony (1987) *Journeys into Bedfordshire*
The Book Castle
Matthews, Rupert (2004) *Haunted Places of Bedfordshire & Buckinghamshire* Countryside Books
O'Dell, Damien (2013) *Paranormal Bedfordshire: True Ghost Stories* Amberley Publishing – revised Kindle edition
Pevsner, Nicholas (1968) *The Buildings of England: Bedfordshire, Huntingdon and Peterborough* Penguin Books

http://therealparanormalx.synthasite.com/haunted-pubs-hotels-bedfordshire.php [accessed June 2018]
http://www.haunted-britain.com/haunted-pubs.htm [accessed July 2018]
http://www.timetravel-britain.com/articles/history/hauntedpubs.shtml [accessed June 2018]
https://www.greeneking.co.uk/newsroom/latest-news/halloween-haunted-pub-guide-stories/ [accessed July 2018]
https://www.stayinapub.co.uk/PlacesToVisit/South_East/Bedfordshire/Why_Bedfordshire [accessed July 2018]

Printed in Great Britain
by Amazon